Broadway
PIANO SOLOS

ISBN 978-1-4234-8140-9

HAL•LEONARD®
CORPORATION
7777 W. BLUEMOUND RD. P.O. BOX 13819 MILWAUKEE, WI 53213

Visit Hal Leonard Online at
www.halleonard.com

ANY DREAM WILL DO

from JOSEPH AND THE AMAZING TECHNICOLOR® DREAMCOAT

Music by ANDREW LLOYD WEBBER
Lyrics by TIM RICE

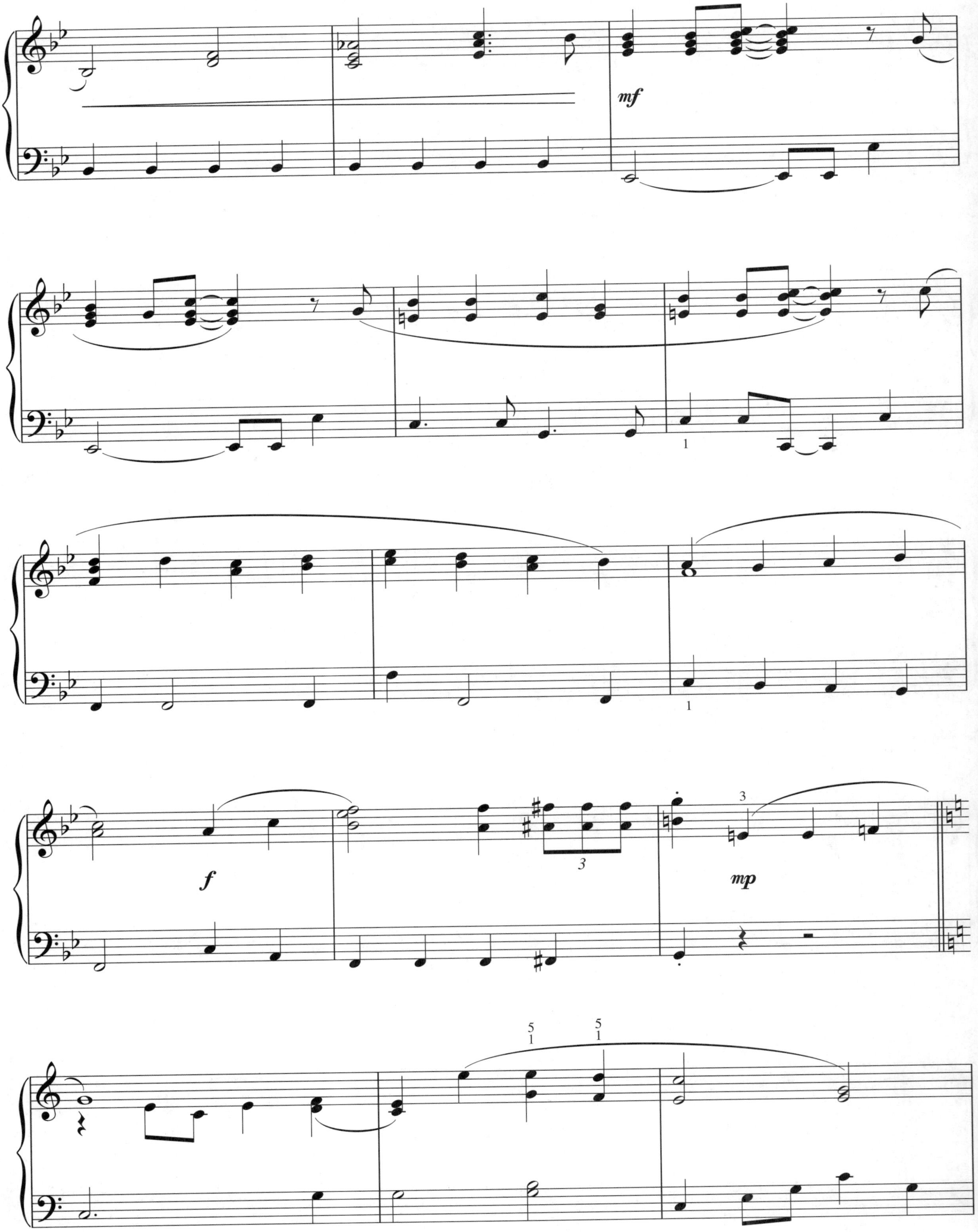
mf
f
mp

BALI HA'I
from SOUTH PACIFIC

Lyrics by OSCAR HAMMERSTEIN II
Music by RICHARD RODGERS

CLIMB EV'RY MOUNTAIN

from THE SOUND OF MUSIC

Lyrics by OSCAR HAMMERSTEIN II
Music by RICHARD RODGERS

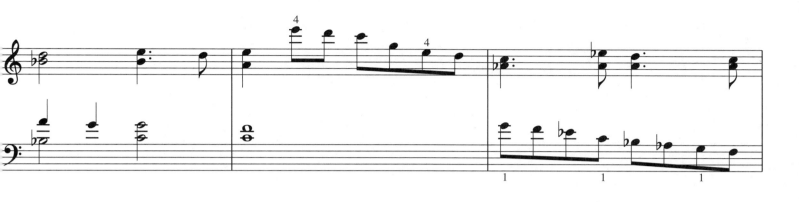

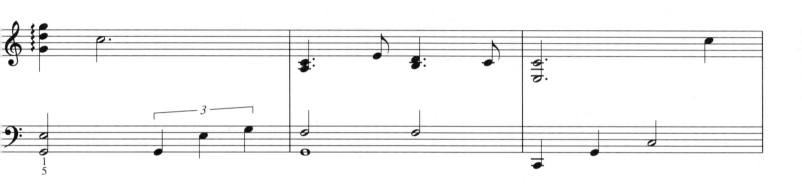

DO YOU HEAR THE PEOPLE SING?

from LES MISÉRABLES

Music by CLAUDE-MICHEL SCHÖNBERG
Lyrics by ALAIN BOUBLIL, JEAN-MARC NATEL and HERBERT KRETZMER

DON'T CRY FOR ME ARGENTINA

from EVITA

Words by TIM RICE
Music by ANDREW LLOYD WEBBER

GETTING TO KNOW YOU

from THE KING AND I

Lyrics by OSCAR HAMMERSTEIN II
Music by RICHARD RODGERS

Gracefully

THE LAST NIGHT OF THE WORLD

from MISS SAIGON

Music by CLAUDE-MICHEL SCHÖNBERG
Lyrics by RICHARD MALTBY JR. and ALAIN BOUBLIL
Adapted from original French Lyrics by ALAIN BOUBLIL

I DON'T KNOW HOW TO LOVE HIM

from JESUS CHRIST SUPERSTAR

Words by TIM RICE
Music by ANDREW LLOYD WEBBER

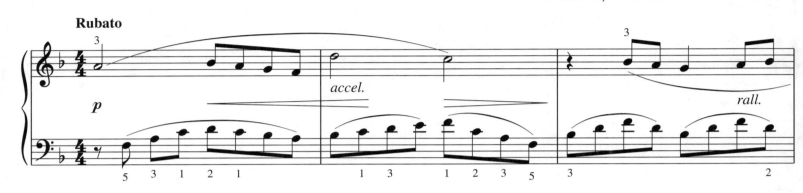

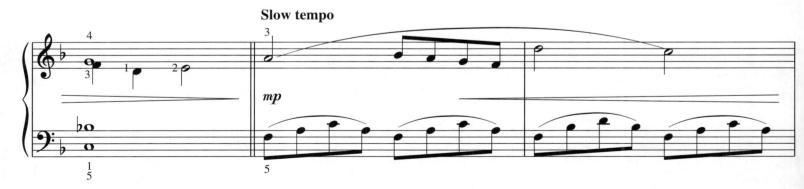

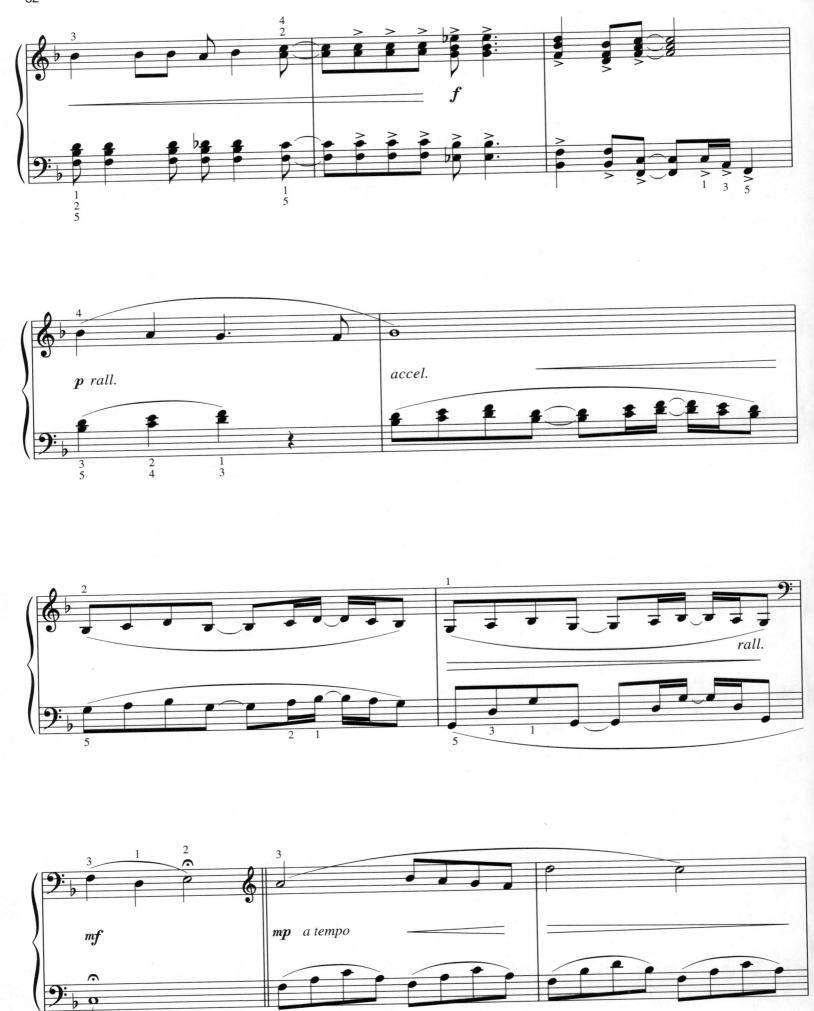

SUPERSTAR
from JESUS CHRIST SUPERSTAR

Words by TIM RICE
Music by ANDREW LLOYD WEBBER

No pedal

Repeat and Fade

THE MUSIC OF THE NIGHT
from THE PHANTOM OF THE OPERA

Music by ANDREW LLOYD WEBBER
Lyrics by CHARLES HART
Additional Lyrics by RICHARD STILGOE

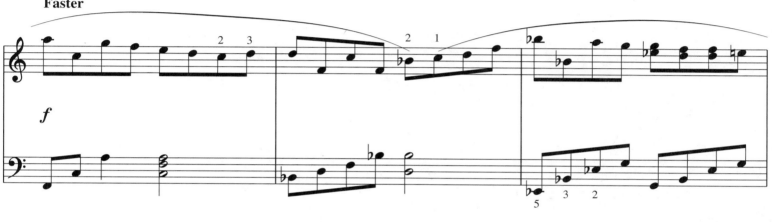

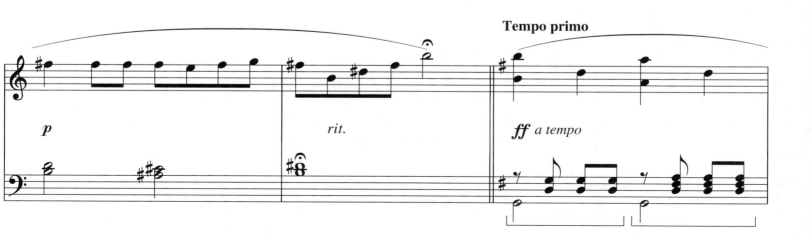

Ped. simile

rit.

p a tempo

rit.

a tempo

pp

ONE
from A CHORUS LINE

Music by MARVIN HAMLISCH
Lyric by EDWARD KLEBAN

THE PHANTOM OF THE OPERA

from THE PHANTOM OF THE OPERA

Music by ANDREW LLOYD WEBBER
Lyrics by CHARLES HART
Additional Lyrics by RICHARD STILGOE
and MIKE BATT

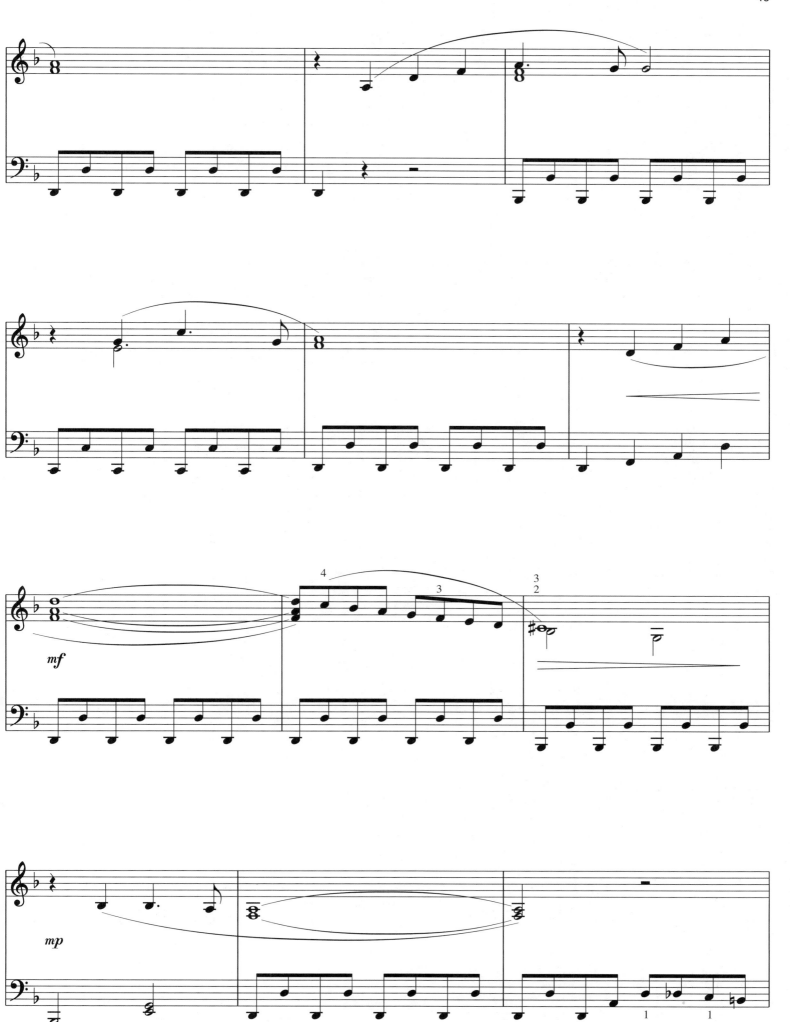

POPULAR
from the Broadway Musical WICKED

Music and Lyrics by
STEPHEN SCHWARTZ

WISHING YOU WERE SOMEHOW HERE AGAIN

from THE PHANTOM OF THE OPERA

Music by ANDREW LLOYD WEBBER
Lyrics by CHARLES HART
Additional Lyrics by RICHARD STILGOE

WONDERFUL
from the Broadway Musical WICKED

Music and Lyrics by
STEPHEN SCHWARTZ

Freely

Slow Ragtime

Faster, light 2

Moderate Ragtime

WHAT I DID FOR LOVE

from A CHORUS LINE

Music by MARVIN HAMLISCH
Lyric by EDWARD KLEBAN

HAL LEONARD:
Your Source for the Best of Broadway

THE BEST BROADWAY SONGS EVER

Over 70 songs from Broadway's latest and greatest hit shows: As Long as He Needs Me • Bess, You Is My Woman • Bewitched • Comedy Tonight • Don't Cry for Me Argentina • Getting to Know You • I Could Have Danced All Night • I Dreamed a Dream • If I Were a Rich Man • The Last Night of the World • Love Changes Everything • Oklahoma • Ol' Man River • People • Try to Remember • and more.
00309155 Piano/Vocal/Guitar..................................$24.95

THE BIG BOOK OF BROADWAY

This edition includes 70 songs from classic musicals and recent blockbusters like *The Producers, Aida* and *Hairspray*. Includes: Bring Him Home • Camelot • Everything's Coming Up Roses • The Impossible Dream • A Lot of Livin' to Do • One • Some Enchanted Evening • Thoroughly Modern Millie • Till There Was You • and more.
00311658 Piano/Vocal/Guitar $19.95

BROADWAY CLASSICS

PIANO PLAY-ALONG SERIES, VOLUME 4
This book/CD pack provides keyboardists with a full performance track and a separate backing track for each tune. Songs include: Ain't Misbehavin' • Cabaret • If I Were a Bell • Memory • Oklahoma • Some Enchanted Evening • The Sound of Music • You'll Never Walk Alone.
00311075 Book/CD Pack $14.95

BROADWAY DELUXE

125 of Broadway's biggest show tunes! Includes such showstoppers as: Bewitched • Cabaret • Camelot • Day by Day • Hello Young Lovers • I Could Have Danced All Night • I Talk to the Trees • I've Grown Accustomed to Her Face • If Ever I Would Leave You • The Lady Is a Tramp • My Heart Belongs to Daddy • Oklahoma • September Song • Seventy Six Trombones • Try to Remember • and more!
00309245 Piano/Vocal/Guitar $24.95

BROADWAY SONGS

Get more bang for your buck with this jam-packed collection of 73 songs from 56 shows, including *Annie Get Your Gun, Cabaret, The Full Monty, Jekyll & Hyde, Les Misérables, Oklahoma* and more. Songs: Any Dream Will Do • Consider Yourself • Footloose • Getting to Know You • I Dreamed a Dream • One • People • Summer Nights • The Surrey with the Fringe on Top • With One Look • and more.
00310832 Piano/Vocal/Guitar...............................$12.95

CONTEMPORARY BROADWAY

44 songs from 25 contemporary musicals and Broadway revivals. Includes: And All That Jazz (*Chicago*) • Dancing Queen (*Mamma Mia!*) • Good Morning Baltimore (*Hairspray*) • Mein Herr (*Cabaret*) • Popular (*Wicked*) • Purpose (*Avenue Q*) • Seasons of Love (*Rent*) • When You Got It, Flaunt It (*The Producers*) • You Rule My World (*The Full Monty*) • and more.
00310796 Piano/Vocal/Guitar..................................$18.95

DEFINITIVE BROADWAY

142 of the greatest show tunes ever, including: Don't Cry for Me Argentina • Hello, Dolly! • I Dreamed a Dream • Lullaby of Broadway • Mack the Knife • Memory • Send in the Clowns • Somewhere • The Sound of Music • Strike Up the Band • Summertime • Sunrise, Sunset • Tea for Two • Tomorrow • What I Did for Love • and more.
00359570 Piano/Vocal/Guitar...................................$24.95

ESSENTIAL SONGS: BROADWAY

Over 100 songs are included in this top-notch collection: Any Dream Will Do • Blue Skies • Cabaret • Don't Cry for Me, Argentina • Edelweiss • Hello, Dolly! • I'll Be Seeing You • Memory • The Music of the Night • Oklahoma • Seasons of Love • Summer Nights • There's No Business like Show Business • Tomorrow • and more.
00311222 Piano/Vocal/Guitar $24.95

KIDS' BROADWAY SONGBOOK

An unprecedented collection of songs originally performed by children on the Broadway stage. Includes 16 songs for boys and girls, including: Gary, Indiana (*The Music Man*) • Castle on a Cloud (*Les Misérables*) • Where Is Love? (*Oliver!*) • Tomorrow (*Annie*) • and more.
00311609 Book Only................................$14.95
00740149 Book/CD Pack...............................$24.99

THE OFF-BROADWAY SONGBOOK

42 gems from off-Broadway hits, including *Godspell, Tick Tick...Boom!, The Fantasticks, Once upon a Mattress, The Wild Party* and more. Songs include: Always a Bridesmaid • Come to Your Senses • Day by Day • Happiness • How Glory Goes • I Hate Musicals • The Picture in the Hall • Soon It's Gonna Rain • Stars and the Moon • Still Hurting • Twilight • and more.
00311168 Piano/Vocal/Guitar $16.95

THE TONY AWARDS SONGBOOK

This collection assembles songs from each of Tony-winning Best Musicals through "Mama Who Bore Me" from 2007 winner *Spring Awakening*. Songs include: Til There Was You • The Sound of Music • Hello, Dolly! • Sunrise, Sunset • Send in the Clowns • Tomorrow • Memory • I Dreamed a Dream • Seasons of Love • Circle of Life • Mama, I'm a Big Girl Now • and more. Includes photos and a table of contents listed both chronologically and alphabetically.
00311092 Piano/Vocal/Guitar $19.95

THE ULTIMATE BROADWAY FAKE BOOK

Over 700 songs from more than 200 Broadway shows! Songs include: All I Ask of You • Bewitched • Cabaret • Don't Cry for Me Argentina • Edelweiss • Getting to Know You • Hello, Dolly! • If I Were a Rich Man • Last Night of the World • The Music of the Night • Oklahoma • People • Seasons of Love • Tell Me on a Sunday • Unexpected Song • and more!
00240046 Melody/Lyrics/Chords.....................$47.50

ULTIMATE BROADWAY PLATINUM

100 popular Broadway songs: As If We Never Said Goodbye • Bye Bye Birdie • Camelot • Everything's Coming Up Roses • Gigi • Hello, Young Lovers • I Enjoy Being a Girl • Just in Time • My Favorite Things • On a Clear Day • People • Sun and Moon • Try to Remember • Who Can I Turn To • Younger Than Springtime • and many more.
00311496 Piano/Vocal/Guitar $22.95

Prices, contents, and availability subject to change without notice.
Some products may not be available outside the U.S.A.

FOR MORE INFORMATION, SEE YOUR LOCAL MUSIC DEALER, OR WRITE TO:

HAL•LEONARD®
CORPORATION

7777 W. BLUEMOUND RD. P.O. BOX 13819 MILWAUKEE, WI 53213

Get complete songlists and more at www.halleonard.com

0209

Classic Collections Of Your Favorite Songs

arranged for piano, voice, and guitar.

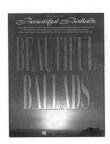

Beautiful Ballads

A massive collection of 87 songs, including: April in Paris • Autumn in New York • Call Me Irresponsible • Cry Me a River • I Wish You Love • I'll Be Seeing You • If • Imagine • Isn't It Romantic? • It's Impossible (Somos Novios) • Mona Lisa • Moon River • People • The Way We Were • A Whole New World (Aladdin's Theme) • and more.
00311679 ....$17.95

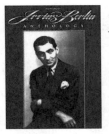

Irving Berlin Anthology

A comprehensive collection of 61 timeless songs with a bio, song background notes, and photos. Songs include: Always • Blue Skies • Cheek to Cheek • God Bless America • Marie • Puttin' on the Ritz • Steppin' Out with My Baby • There's No Business Like Show Business • White Christmas • (I Wonder Why?) You're Just in Love • and more.
00312493 ....$22.95

The Big Book of Standards

86 classics essential to any music library, including: April in Paris • Autumn in New York • Blue Skies • Cheek to Cheek • Heart and Soul • I Left My Heart in San Francisco • In the Mood • Isn't It Romantic? • Mona Lisa • Moon River • The Nearness of You • Out of Nowhere • Spanish Eyes • Star Dust • Stella by Starlight • That Old Black Magic • They Say It's Wonderful • What Now My Love • and more.
00311667 ....$19.95

Broadway Deluxe

This exciting collection of 125 of Broadway's biggest show tunes is deluxe indeed! Includes such showstoppers as: Bewitched • Cabaret • Camelot • Day by Day • Hello Young Lovers • I Could Have Danced All Night • I've Grown Accustomed to Her Face • If Ever I Would Leave You • The Lady Is a Tramp • I Talk to the Trees • My Heart Belongs to Daddy • Oklahoma • September Song • Seventy Six Trombones • Try to Remember • and more!
00309245 ....$24.95

The Great American Songbook – The Singers

Crooners, wailers, shouters, balladeers: some of our greatest pop vocalists have poured their hearts and souls into the musical gems of the Great American Songbook. This folio features 100 of these classics by Louis Armstrong, Tony Bennett, Rosemary Clooney, Nat "King" Cole, Bing Crosby, Doris Day, Ella Fitzgerald, Judy Garland, Dean Martin, Frank Sinatra, Barbra Streisand, Mel Tormé, and others.
00311433 ....$24.95

I'll Be Seeing You: 50 Songs of World War II

A salute to the music and memories of WWII, including a year-by-year chronology of events on the homefront, dozens of photos, and 50 radio favorites of the GIs and their families back home, including: Boogie Woogie Bugle Boy • Don't Sit Under the Apple Tree (With Anyone Else But Me) • I Don't Want to Walk Without You • I'll Be Seeing You • Moonlight in Vermont • There's a Star-Spangled Banner Waving Somewhere • You'd Be So Nice to Come Home To • and more.
00311698 ....$19.95

Lounge Music – 2nd Edition

Features over 50 top requests of the martini crowd: All the Way • Fever • I Write the Songs • Misty • Moon River • That's Amore (That's Love) • Yesterday • more.

00310193 ....$15.95

Best of Cole Porter

38 of his classics, including: All of You • Anything Goes • Be a Clown • Don't Fence Me In • I Get a Kick Out of You • In the Still of the Night • Let's Do It (Let's Fall in Love) • Night and Day • You Do Something to Me • and many more.

00311577 ....$14.95

Big Band Favorites

A great collection of 70 of the best Swing Era songs, including: East of the Sun • Honeysuckle Rose • I Can't Get Started with You • I'll Be Seeing You • In the Mood • Let's Get Away from It All • Moonglow • Moonlight in Vermont • Opus One • Stompin' at the Savoy • Tuxedo Junction • more!
00310445 ....$16.95

The Best of Rodgers & Hammerstein

A capsule of 26 classics from this legendary duo. Songs include: Climb Ev'ry Mountain • Edelweiss • Getting to Know You • I'm Gonna Wash That Man Right Outta My Hair • My Favorite Things • Oklahoma • The Surrey with the Fringe on Top • You'll Never Walk Alone • and more.
00308210 ....$16.95

The Best Songs Ever – 5th Edition

Over 70 must-own classics, including: All I Ask of You • Body and Soul • Crazy • Fly Me to the Moon • Here's That Rainy Day • Imagine • Love Me Tender • Memory • Moonlight in Vermont • My Funny Valentine • People • Satin Doll • Save the Best for Last • Tears in Heaven • A Time for Us • The Way We Were • What a Wonderful World • When I Fall in Love • and more.
00359224 ....$22.95

Torch Songs

Sing your heart out with this collection of 59 sultry jazz and big band melancholy masterpieces, including: Angel Eyes • Cry Me a River • I Can't Get Started • I Got It Bad and That Ain't Good • I'm Glad There Is You • Lover Man (Oh, Where Can You Be?) • Misty • My Funny Valentine • Stormy Weather • and many more! 224 pages.
00490446 ....$17.95